For Martha & Richard
and
For Rosalind

Pigeon

Roland Flint

PIGEON

North Carolina Wesleyan College Press

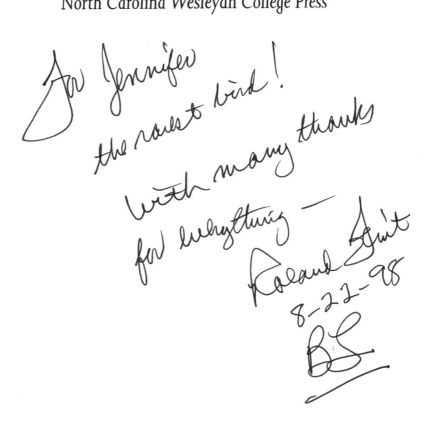

For Jennifer
the rarest bird!
with many thanks
for everything —
Roland Flint
8-22-98

LC 91-62198

ISBN 0-933598-30-0 (regular edition)
ISBN 0-933598-31-9 (signed)

Some of these poems have appeared in
the following magazines and journals:
Hubbub, Poet Lore, TriQuarterly, and
Willamette Journal. Ten have appeared
in Resuming Green (1983).

This project is supported by a grant
from the National Endowment of the
Arts in Washington D.C., a Federal
Agency

Published by
North Carolina Wesleyan College Press
3400 North Wesleyan Boulevard
Rocky Mount, North Carolina
27804

Contents

He Didn't Know He Was A   ix

I

Sitting In A Light As Beautiful   3
On February 24 Pigeon   4
One June In His New Home   5
God Bless Invention, Pigeon   6
Pigeon's Knee Goes   7
So One Day Pigeon   8
Pigeon Chortles   9
Nearing Their Official   11

II

After Writing 28 Days Without A Pause   15
What A Way To End   16
Suddenly Goddamned Tired Of Poets   17
But To Pigeon Hosting Poets, Zimmer   19
While Pigeon Is (Modestly)   20
Writing Those Long-Line Poems Pigeon   21
An Editor From Buzzard Press Writes   22
Pigeon Sees How This Scratching Of His   23

III

Pigeon Is Happiest   27
Pigeon Saw (He Guesses)   28
To The Only Absolute Beauty Someone   29

Pigeon Saw Siv   30
In NYC, After Deciding Not   31
O Connie, Pigeon's Bill   32
Pigeon Remembers Abruptly   33
October Is Becoming His Favorite   34

IV

Pigeon Wonders Again   37
Pigeon Is Jealous After Seeing   38
As On Most Days, On His Birthday Pigeon   39
When Noisily Yelling Pigeon   40
Pigeon All Day   42
Pigeon Wakes Stiff In The Night   43
No Sooner Is Pigeon   44
Pigeon In The Night   45

V

Pigeon Can't Remember   49
Re-reading Conrad Pigeon   51
At The Graduation Parties Pigeon   52
Pigeon Defies The Moon   53
Grateful Pigeon In A Flash   54
Pigeon Is A Little   55
Under Pressure Pigeon Stops Fighting It   56
When Her Digital Clock   57

He Didn't Know He was A

Pigeon: until the day in New York City
When he'd left the rented nest & her
He's often called a nest & was walking,
Bad hungover from the pre-wedding bash
To his favorite Wolf's (52nd & 7th)
For bagel, egg & aspirin,
And his path was blocked by
Pigeons & then just one,
Fat, rumpled, grouchy, clumsy,
And he & the pigeon did
A little dance before finding
The paths around, & he thought,
Oh God, I danced like that last night
At the fancy dinner, dressed just
Like a pigeon in the rented tux,
Colliding with the bride's mother,
Saying some dumb pigeon-yiddish, & pigeon
Dancing, drunk & bumbling,
Stumbling by: pigeon, plain
As pigeon.

I

Sitting in *A Light As Beautiful*

As Gabriel Conroy dreamed
His secret life away in, pigeon
In love in his new living
Room one Wednesday afternoon
Figures something (little) out:
He could sit like this forever,
For the Rest Of It, it feels so good,
The sun's cello blousing the curtains—
But he would brood a slippage from his roost.
Meanwhile time is on him
Thursday & Friday, Saturday & Sunday
All so close & closely planned it's
As if they're over now, &
Pigeon figures the only way
To make a little hole in time
Is by this scratch, how good or bad
Give over, the only sure survivor,
A pigeon down at last. So:
When he's not trying at least to fly
A mote is in his eye
As steady dependable time
Makes its black hole in him.

On February 24 Pigeon

Is, like Henry, "up for good at 5"
And it is their 1st anniversary
To sing a small thing about: but
He and the lady for some reason
Have had a bad night at sleeping
Into their anniversary & pigeon
Thinks he knows why: because the flu
All week has had them
Only reading in bed & actually
Sleeping together (mostly). Rare
For L&p, this continence & unwoods pecker.
As Roethke's dancing grizzly says:
"Who reads in bed fornicates on the stove."
Or Berryman: whose "lass is braking,"
His "brass is aching." So . . . late into
The night, very literary p is reading
Arch & undisguisedly clever Updike,
His review of Flaubert's letters,
While a pigeon pie is baking
In the furnace out behind.
And when those furnaces behind
Have you banking till you're blind
You may rage like Robert Burton,
Or, sans pintle, Thomas Merton.

One June In His New Home

While pigeon is making a little scratch
These days against the great white
Emptiness of page times age &
While he is more & more at home
In his present new roost & corner,
He thinks he should have flown the coop
To Yaddo or Ossabaw or MacDowell or Millay
Or Sweet Briar or Taos or Hambidge or some place,
To make a clean break—
From school & rule from trouble & strife
The everyday birds & turds the ids & kids—
Apollo to Hermes a little.
He seems to need the grip of gypsy
Once a year or so to keep him straight on
The crooked path he means to fly,
To avoid locking up in,
As master Wystan says,
A social science or long views.
(So runs, at least, the late excuse.)

God Bless Invention, Pigeon

Says, because,
When his lady's broken thigh
Was, though mending, muscle-knotted
Like a fist (her size)
And, as she lay beside him,
After dinner having tea,
Kneading it gingerly with her left hand,
Then invention came a little,
Giving him the metal teapot,
Hot but not too hot (through the sheet)
To iron the knot out, steady & hard,
Agitato ma non troppo,
For half an hour.
Pigeon says God bless it because
Her leg felt better all night
To let her sleep, for a change,
And also bless invention for
The ways she rubbed him back:
Now there's a rub, by God.
God bless it too—& does.

Pigeon's Knee Goes

Pop! when he's jogging & he
Almost trips on the stone or root
But still he jogs his (wobble) jog
An hour or more, &
It isn't till later climbing stairs
That it Pops! again, this time for
Real, knows tumbling p,
Who wraps it in heat a while &
Tries to do some loosening exercise.
It will not bend. So pigeon
Doesn't hit his knees to pray tonight
As, in his way, he always usually does.
So most unpigeon lady must
Pigeon (oremus) for both:
They save the knee to pray, & vary,
When she's the (darling) missionary.

So One Day Pigeon

Defied his own advice for years,
The odds against the death of grief,
And, to say it, got
Married:
With only the Judge
And Peggy & Harvey, retreads too,
To witness & watch with nestlings
Newly sibbed, approving (?)
Bubbling along beside,
Champagne, a wheel of brie,
Strawberries red & big & sweet,
Even a wedding cake: then
Standing between the judge & the chimney
Pigeon & lady say right here is where.
Let any bless who care. Next,
Pigeon's voice goes warbly as he sings
What he has meant & planned,
But hasn't first warned anyone:
How can I live without thee, how forgo
He would declare and could himself believe—
Songs by his betters to bless
The altered happiness.

Pigeon Chortles

Over their statistics:
Physicians do it 1.7 times per week,
Executives 1.6, farmers 1.1,
According to the Sunday Supplement.
Let's see, sings chortling pigeon,
To his bride (of seven years),
That means 17 times in 10 weeks,
Or 16 or 11! depending on your work.
(What brings up the doctor's average?—
Psychiatricks?—or nurses?)
And if they admit to such sad figures,
What's the truth? says doubting p.
Pigeon gets out his pocket calculator to see that
Medics get 88.4 a year,
And remembers another folk-joke
He & his bride defy:
Put a penny in a jar every time the first year,
Take one out every time, thereafter,
And you'll *never* empty it.
And they remember the angry friend at a party
Complaining about this moron of a woman
Writing in an anti-feminist book
That you should sex your old man every day,
"For God's *sake!*" How awful!
Sad (a little) for the struggling rest,

Pigeon & lady home again nestle,
Letting the nest decide them how
They will not take
The two-year break
Their stats allow.

Nearing Their Official

First Anniversary pigeon remembers
What was, maybe, their first one,
Unofficial, when they were a year
In flesh, or so, but new in love,
Or, anyway, the pigeon's lady knew it
(So she says) & pigeon was starting to suspect,
At least, that this was it.
Nearing this date six years later
Pigeon thinks she is the only girl in the
Truest sense he's ever had:
For nests & bests & bads & all,
The firsts for each enough
Despite the other lives & (partial) many loves,
And saying it reminds him of that day
Six years or so ago when she
Was telling him of her home, New Zealand:
South Island, North Island, Maoris,
Mori-oris, geysers, glaciers, green mountains & steam,
And how, small as it is, & known,
"There are still parts," she said,
Blushing a little & looking up to him like a question,
That he should understand it to be literal, "there *are*
Still parts of the country no one has explored."
In New Zealand secrets of the heart they go,
Lady & pigeon, & find it so.

II

After Writing Twenty-eight Days Without A Pause

Pigeon skipped a day & woke
With childhood feelings of, he'll call it,
Giantism, as he lay too full
And half-boozed still
All the massy old enormous pressure
On his wings which felt
To pigeon in the dark
Pterodactyl at least, the
Claws he rubbed together or
Scrubbed the perch with even bigger
And pigeon trying not to ignore it,
Sleep it away as when he was little,
Scared, but trying now to hold it,
Stay to see what it is:
Memory of birthing in the
Clotted channel—*squeezed. . .*?
Source of pigeon claustrophobia for sure.
It's a feeling pigeon hadn't had for
Fifteen, twenty years & which
Used to be very bad: moon or beach on pigeon
Little. But is probably also related
To his impulse, solo, to turn off
The elevator lights, grasp the waist-high
Railing in his claws & perching dream,
As down the sliding dark,
Pigeon flies the sea.

What A Way to End

The best month of all,
Thinks pigeon: with no
Scratch. Nothing
All day the last day of
The brightest October of all,
Except four million nine hundred thousand
And eighty-five freshman papers (to track—
By noon—in pigeon blood all over) & despite
All the new perches & swan
(Well almost swan) dives already done.
So pigeon just dedicates this one
To October the Thirty First,
A Retrospective Trickle.
(Here's November, pumpkin bright—
He greets it with a Dickel.)

Suddenly Goddamned Tired of Poets

Pigeon sulks, brooding about the limey,
His poet-visit, demanding lunch for 3,
A tape, please, of his reading,
An office-line on which to call
"A couple of places"—*free* is understood—
"New York?"—OK, says p, "Minneapolis?"—eh. . .
OK, "London?" ah, no, says p,
Knowing who will pay for these
And finding his craw (or stones) at last.
Also: can you pick me up put me up
Carry my bags sell my books
Buy my books, get my check, get it cashed,
Change the readers change the order change it back
See me off check the flight drive me there—no!
The other airport! 40 miles away!
Confirm my ticket check my bags pay the freight—
Hoping it's not too much trouble?
The while insinuating pigeon is remiss
In hosting, not offering as he had
To the bloody limey's human if limey pal
Martinis after at his house & cheese & Juniors
To feast a party look (at least) upon. . . .
Anyway he has to wing right back to London
Where, he says, the media are dying for him,
Because of the POETRY OLYMPICS he just ran,

Starring him and Corso, at Westminster Abbey,
And he must go hold Corso's hand on telly,
Beard the canny press & maybe make a decent guinea
Before anapesting off to Cotswolds rural.
So . . . it turns out later—
He should not have been left alone
With the pigeon's trusting phone
On which he made not 2 calls but 7—one to LA
And, you guessed it, one to London,
All charged to guess whose pigeon?
It nearly makes him forget that
The reading was (OK—OK) ok.

But To Pigeon Hosting Poets, Zimmer

Is another story, paying his own parking,
Offering hard cash at lunch (which pigeon's
Boss is paying for), bringing along his wife
So not assuming his fee includes
All the sophomores he can eat & reading
To the minute what pigeon asked him to.
Considerate also of the limey
(Who insists on reading last),
Charming pigeon's & every ear
(Excepting maybe the limey's) who hear
The simple complicated songs,
Beer-belly magic waving its wand—
Ah, the jampacked room was Zimmer when he started
Zimmer when he stopped
And even as the limey read
The room was solid Zimmer.
Twice now pigeon hosting Zimmer
Has stuck him with a poet
Who blows braver louder longer but is dimmer
And he swears, by God, next time he will atone
By having immer Zimmer read (2 hours) alone.

While Pigeon Is (Modestly)

Barding off in Mount Vernon
To the ladies (mostly, elderly) of
The Poetry Society of Virginia
(For whiskey-sour punch, lunch,
A $150 fee & $41.25 in booksales)
In D.C. the Big Stuff is going on at the Folger:
Hollander & Howard & Davies & Bloom
And Perloff & Merwin & Plumly,
All slavering the age's Ashbery as
Our "best and most representative," I guess,
Since Stevens anyway:
Hauling off one at a time,
Reeling like drunks from a furnace, gone
On the ink-blue wine of self-regard,
Mumbling and grumbling clinamen toast
Or carving up Lucifer's roast.
So pigeon at 45 is tired of
Hegemonies of stone, hub-caps from New Haven
Letting us know *What's It*, how plumbly.
OK: pigeon at 45 admits he's steamed
How few the bigs have read his stuff at all
And wishes he could believe it *is* a daisy chain
You need to break a link to,
But he's not cynic here—or *more* a cynic?—
Thinking it's mostly blindness and sleep-walking
And the terrible number of pigeonless songs,
Much less who's vamping whom,
As pearl off empires bloom.

20

Writing Those Long-Line Poems Pigeon

(Pre-pigeon) *never* thought someday he'd try
Couplets again: he thought he'd found the way
To write his song forever, turning the page
Around, side-ways, letting it go, no hedge
Of rhyme or meter to crank him in,
Only the end of the yellow legal-sheet to turn
It at the end of *sentences: they* made
The pigeon learn to pull & bend it till it's said.
Now nothing but flies easier from his hand
(Or claw) than *these*, rag-wingéd contraband.

An Editor From Buzzard Press Writes

To the pigeon saying thanks for sending
The poems as requested: we're shooting 7 back,
But one we "really like,"
And enclose a copy with a "number of changes"
"We think would make the poem stronger."
It's a little (28-line) versicle pigeon
Worked his tail off on (as usual) &
These guys suggest 21 changes! 21!
Including striking out half a line, then
A whole line, most of the definite articles—
Like any hapless rookie—& then,
The worst to p, they *rewrite* a line, providing
A bird-brained metaphor of their own,
Changing the line utterly, removing a meaning
Pigeon planted with ordinary, obsessed, & off-hand care.
Fuck you very much in his reply says (r)aging p,
But grinning with integrity.

Pigeon Sees How This Scratching Of His

Will be more & more the center:
Family & friends he loves are dying
Of hearts or falling, pills or cancer,
And as long as pigeon is staying
On behind (& long he means & wants
To do) he must always court & chance
The dumbest failures of saying
(Almost) exactly what he means. He's not praying
For miracles or lost in some delusion
He'll get out alive, nor even (for long) survive:
This ugly place he loves in rapt confusion.

III

Pigeon Is Happiest

When the room is filled with people,
Drinking & talking or sitting down to food—
All the room filled up with what
The pigeon loves to feed on: especially smart
Folks, their talk about poems or genetics, say,
Or Wittgenstein's *Investigations*, all which
(Except some poems) p knows nothing of
But hears & recognizes *shapes* he knows
In all of them, a little persistent song
At the center of each, to him the metaphor
That makes it as it makes it go
And makes the pigeon in his hosting glow.
No wonder if they take a shine to him,
Who tries whatever wobbles up to shim.

Pigeon Saw (He Guesses)

A freshwoman girl, little,
Slender & pretty
With brown hair soft at her shoulders,
Blue eyes lighting her smile
And she was talking to a boy
Almost as new. It was nothing
Important, thinks p, &
It was everything:
How they'll try this & that,
Maybe, if things work out, & what
They'll some day get & have to do.
She wears those charming ugly clogs,
Stands pigeon-toed, a knee turning in,
In her jeans, looking the smallest bird.
He can't quite see the boy from here
But loves them both, yes,
Against the future grazing.

To The Only Absolute Beauty Someone

Is sending roses anonymously
And pigeon wishes it were he—
Oh maybe you know (by your light)
A beauty *you* think perfect, but
The pigeon doubts, trusting his eye,
There is another one like this: no vellums
Or oven-bread or delicacy from flax
Can take a flesh this tone,
No metaphor to gather hair up in the back so
Soft, thick, auburn-red &
Radiantly sexed withal,
Spain in the blood some place, & a nun, & Capri.
And hilarious to p, she doesn't know:
He sees she thinks she's bone and ghost,
A certain flash to men. Well listen:
General Motors & NASA,
And all the nuclear power plants, the temples,
The cloud-capped towers
And the great globe itself could buzz
A year at least if we could turn
Libido that burns for her
(Or has) to lignite or uranium or
The blood-black oil of ancient birds,
From whom, irrelevantly,
Descends at last admiring p,
Who thinks, by God, *somebody* knows
The perfect flower for her, blood-red: *a rose.*

Pigeon Saw Siv

Again, saw her who makes him
(Who not?) crazy to ruffle her nest
To buzz her hedges curdle her cream
With or without a sieve to taste,
To tread & trestle to boogie & wrestle—
What a beauty! the grand wide gold
Brown eyes, the brown thick red & blonde long hair,
Mixed natural, like curls ablaze the crown,
To foxfire three or four feet down,
Down the gorgeous 6' smorgasbord,
Striking dumb as pigeons all
Who look on her the first time—
As when he saw her across the wide room,
Seeming to look back, seeming to be
Walking towards him, smiling like an eclipse,
Coming to kiss him warmly on the mouth
And say, a flicka doubt,
"You are James Wright?"
Another reason to wish it.
But he's Daffy Duck when she's around—
And pigeon for the rest by pigeons bound.

In NYC, After Deciding Not

To call her, a sweet old flame
He used to call the robin,
And after writing, as well, 2
Pigeons about fidelity, pigeon
Gets off the subway at 50th & 7th
On his way to the Picasso show & meets
Her, striding down 7th to work,
Beautiful & strong & older
And both are startled & happy &
Have coffee & talk before off they fly
Forever again & she doesn't embarrass p
By asking how long he's been in town
(Without calling, etc.) or why.
Pigeon is unconfused at last to say
He loves her and he loves his bride,
Faithful to each in her way.
And he thinks he loves (yes) others too—
Confusions of love abide.

O Connie, Pigeon's Bill

Glistens & waters
At your invitation to dinner.
He scrubs & drums it
On his appointment book
Like a woodpecker.
What big round wonders, O,
He expects, knowing you,
Hors d'oeuvres to Dessert,
Salmon coming between,
Naturally salted from the sea,
Technicolor flesh of it, and
Perfect circles of Scallop,
Garlic for Gulliver, Tomatoes,
Many Plump Breads to break
The crisp tans of by hand,
Glaciers & Cities of Lettuce,
French Brandy & Candies at the end,
Exquisite chocolate around the nuts—
Pigeon accepts on the Fly!

Pigeon Remembers Abruptly

Six or seven years after their split,
And with deep if complicated pleasure,
How in all his life only she has called him "Dear,"
An old fashioned way in itself to endear.
It must have started before the early
Trouble, &, no doubt, after a while, mere habit,
But he is moved to remember, even so,
Through much of it, she called him "Dear,"
And hopes he was, sometimes at least, to her,
As she is to him this morning, very dear,

October Is Becoming His Favorite

Pigeon thinks, sitting at his perch,
Scratching for the record one of all the
Moments of a dying year: & guessing why,
The worst month of all just by,
He loves October so, is songs,
The high trees, the amplifying leaves
Scorched pumpkin or berry for harvest or wheat,
The whole world by season in movement of
October winds: lifting color from the trees,
Leaves up off the ground & new love,
In old pigeon, whom wind & colors sing.
Or if he loves it all selfishly for
The harvests more by more it means to him,
How five days of October cannot go by
Without his consulting the old dark
About their deal, without a plain try
At days & nights & what comes flying by.

IV

Pigeon Wonders Again

If an ordinary pigeon can
Make a nest to last forever.
OK, not forever really or even
Within three or four
Methuselahs of Hector but
Till Thursday, say, or
The end of the summer, century or so.
Whether it's possible on the tops of low
Buildings or in open eaves, old-house cupolas,
To make, with sticks & strings & glues,
Saliva for stickum &
Essential if deliberate dirt,
Something for comfort, lying
Down in, hatching, eventually,
All the rest.
And how it all might look from there:
Green & good, thinks pigeon.
No wonder
At all, it's time to go down again
And do the pigeon things.

Pigeon Is Jealous After Seeing

A cardinal this morning—
What red thinks graying pigeon,
Moving like a brush stroke
Zip like that through the trees
And stopping & sitting on a branch where
Only sleepless pigeon saw—earliest morning
To give a light & no one else around
But waddle-jogging pigeon. Flying,
It was a red streak
But when it dandled
In the twig ends of that branch
It puffed like a smaller pigeon,
Squatty, imperious, slow,
An old man waking in a
Red night-shirt, peaked cap,
And sitting up so quick the springs
Work some, like a branch, saying
"Who's that? How come?"
Then back to sleep so still
In October's twigs it looks
Like they are flying.

As On Most Days, On His Birthday Pigeon

Rises early, if 3:41 a.m. to you is,
As even to him it's very, early—though
He's often up before & oftener is
Sleepless & reading an hour or 2 before that:
On this morning, having finished the 47th year,
And starting out on 48, pigeon
Has (he hopes) a thing to say:
Since he got back from Xmas travels
To Zurich & Sofia & Athens, to
Karachi, Bangkok, Hong Kong & Singapore,
To Auckland, Rotorua, Masterton, Wellington,
Christchurch, Honolulu, Los Angeles . . . ,
It's been a bad year for pigeons.
He has never seen so many down,
Dead, frozen in the streets—
None as Dylan doesn't say
But all of their fires out.
And he wonders if there's a campaign
To poison them, these clumsy semblables
He's liking less (to reason the need),
And wonders too if maybe something's
Somehow in his feeder too, causing him little
On the eve of 48 to pigeon for or treble up.

When Noisily Yelling Pigeon

(Stopped at the red light)
Asks the foreman-looking guy,
Hey, is this a Metro-construction, or. . . ?
The man—busy eyeing a drain pipe,
Standing half in & out a door of
The ply-wood walls around the site—says huh?
Looks up & asks it louder, Huh? So p
Repeats, & as the guy steps out to answer
He catches the heel of thick rubber-boots
On the bottom of the rough-cut door-frame &
Nearly takes a header. So close that p & lady
Pull their shoulders back to help,
P catches his breath & squeezes the wheel,
But he flails & grabs the air & rights himself,
And comes up red-faced, grouchy: yes it is a Metro site,
No it ain't a station, just a hole
To dig a tunnel to the station.
Wishing the light would change, p asks—
Because the man seems waiting, looking pissed—
Ah . . . what station? He yells, Peterson & Row
(Or something) giving the name of the construction co.,
Looking redder & less & less sober. Thanks,
Says unclutching & moving p,
As the light at last goes green,

The foreman waving his hand no sweat, &
Heading back to his drain or bottle.
Now it is many days & still memory slow-
Motions the fall, the heel-catch & tumble,
And clawing & muscle-jerked save,
Each time sacking p's shoulders,
Catching his breath, pulling back at the wheel:
Remembering how easy to fumble
Familiar doors, red-faced or drunk, to feel
Thick-heeled & stupid, & stumble.

Pigeon All Day

Had been thinking of his brother,
On his mind & in his
Vague, prophetic heart, so
When the brother's wife called
To say he had come through
A wicked spinal surgery, pigeon knew,
As soon as she said hello, the call was bad
(Though the first he'd heard
Of the condition or cutting).
And scared pigeon hung there shaking
On the neuron down from Maine
As long as he could stand it, learning
What had been b(r)othering him all day.
And he's reminded again
How many deaths would (worse than) kill him:
Like some others this one more.

Pigeon Wakes Stiff In The Night

As usual, of wing & thing,
Unusually of heart with,
Instantly, limber recollection
Of the lovely past one day
When two children were all alive,
Beautiful & strong & running
Down the park in front of him
Into the setting sun,
Their hair, especially the boy's,
Like foxes' as they ran
Catching the red departing day.
All is changed now, even pigeon's love
Is setting darker than it was,
Unbending as his aging knees,
And no nest again, thinks sleepy
But wide awake pigeon,
No nest ever again like that.
Back to the rounded night.

No Sooner Is Pigeon

Coming back some from his loved friend's death,
Greeting the day again, scratching around, &
News comes another old friend is dead,
Bringing the year's total to four from cancer alone.
And so the pigeon flies northwest to be there,
His heart aburst with emptiness to witness
His poor old friend all dead & coffined
To comfort as well as he can the widow & child
To carry his friend to the terrible hole
To eat & drink too much (with grief to blame it on)
To visit his aging parents
To take them out to dinner
To cut his broken-wristed father's steak
To stay two days & nights & mow his mother's lawn
To speak carefully with them of the bereaved
To toss all night in the creaking bed
In which he was conceived.

Pigeon In The Night

Feels a little black hole in his chest
And knows it to be his heart,
Dense with the gravid night,
A black invisible diamond weighing in
With the cruel impacted build-up, the loss
Especially this morning, drawing all the others into it,
Of his own right hand his heart itself,
For a while, his son gone forever.
He can't quite hang on to pigeon when
The night bores in like this.

V

Pigeon Can't Remember

Though it was only yesterday,
If he spent $369.58 to fix his car or
$358.69 & that's a clue how these days go,
Even if he can usually remember whether
"It snowed for 6 days & 6 nights when he was 12"
Or "12 days & 12 nights when he was 6": that's
What's been happening all year,
The every day & far away realities breaking so
He loses names of ones he has loved
Or greatly liked at least, but still, as usual,
Has up so floating many lines down. Well,
Anyway, he spent a chunk on his 10 year-old Valiant
But still it cuts him dead at every stop.
And when he says how come, the fixit guy
Says the manifold's tore up, all cracked,
I didn't see it till too late—no
The tune-up & other stuff didn't fix it,
But hey—it ain't my fault. I'm up to here.
The pigeon tries himself to line it with furnace cement:
No go, of course. Later he has a dream
From which he wakes to think of Brando's saying,
"I got a prostate like a potateh
But I'm still a prutty good stick-man."

Here's the dream:
He's trying to plug the drippy underside
Of a tea-kettle's spout by freezing some water
Into the hole—no go, of course.
What hath time & Valiant pigeon wrought:
Manifolds, heaters, plugs & head-bolts shot.

Re-reading Conrad, Pigeon

Comes to admire after 5 or 6 readings
The Secret Sharer for its crazy
Correspondences & has his own
Interpretation: the sharer is Poland
And its language:
It kills the captain if it stays &
He has to kill it when it goes & so
He does, leaving Captain English sailing home.
OK? Simple, huh? & it makes him grin to see
What Conrad's failure of
(English) laughter can betray:
"On my suggestion," says the captain,
About the murderer he's hiding in his cabin,
"On my suggestion he remained
Almost entirely in the bathroom,
Which, upon the whole, was the safest place."
Pigeon copies out the sentence so, on a note-card,
And shows it to his 14-year-old daughter
(No failure at all in laughter),
Saying to her only, "What's wrong here?"
And, *instantly,* she says, eyes bright,
"*Hole* is spelled wrong—right?"

At The Graduation Parties Pigeon

Has, mostly, a good time,
Drinking a lot of the (surprise)
Too strong punch, jollying parents & being
To the grads a character or gaffer
(He can't always tell), but to some a favorite.
And to those the pigeon realizes he has become
That specific example he brays about
And is surprised all over again which kids
Are eager to say, This is the one, Ma.
From his favorites this pleases him
Excessively, even as he thinks,
Compared to his own old heroes, he
Does *not* measure up: "Thus may poor fools
Believe false teachers." But he
Also sees it doesn't matter, if
(By his grave & pigeon-middling competence),
Like his old heroes to him many years agone,
He has made these think of excellence.
Gaudeamus!

Pigeon Defies The Moon

Its baleful, full-faced glare &
Glares right back, high in the
Laces of cirrus, stratus, featherly
Breaking cumulus, in the
Lignite-blue & deep-night sea.
It is so beautiful to his & him,
Framed by the trees they (sort of) own
In their yard in middle Maryland,
He wants to move it back or stop it
All where it is for a while, the dreaming
Clouds, the many shapes they see in it—
"Attracted to the moon," says she,
And clouds *are* swimming to, around & by it,
So fast it just has time when covered
To make its small moonrises & moonsets,
Especially beautiful & quick over
The sculpted & breaking cumuli.
So pigeon stares right back to see
How it makes up this oldest song: &
Night-struck pigeon facing up
To it, as usual, loses
Trying to compose the night
The way the moon does.

Grateful Pigeon In A Flash

Realizes there's a pot of gold
At the end of the rainbow
Because it's a dream of color times money &
Gold is what all cash & colors come to,
Go from, & signify together:
Refract the light & you get rainbow, bend
It back, to airy thinness, say,
And you twist it thereby back to gold.
And he finds it chromatically on the money,
Because the sun, that pot of gold,
Brings rainbow & morning to light—
By cashing new color for old.

Pigeon Is A Little

(But deeply) annoyed,
Reading over & thinking about
These pigeons, at all the implied
Self-love, -approval, -forgiveness,
In spite of his hating pigeons & all,
Because this particular bird knows
Himself to be a compulsive meddler, needler & nag,
Especially with the little & small,
But also more than now & then
Even with her: all caritas.
While he, like a household nixon,
Tunes into every minutest detail
Especially what the children do
At table or play, at home, TV or away
And needles & nags & carps & bullies, &
Sorry in seconds as he (almost always) is,
In minutes he is doing it again,
Right after (sometimes during) the pigeon apology—
All this on top of being
Vain grouchy boastful & proud—
And not less so for saying them aloud.
On Independence Day, 1980,
For the 2000th time he vows
To tune his instrument & atone,
Especially leaving the little
And better than well enough alone.

Under Pressure Pigeon Stops Fighting It

And gives thanks to the great darkness
Before which he is stupid & reverent,
The sung silence to every question
He no longer asks, wide-eyed, in those cupolas
On the night he roosts in, content,
But frightened still: & prays his heart out
It won't test him in that final way
He has addressed the dark about
In gravest secret, darkest doubt,
Because with all his heart he fears
That test (another time) could break
In half or more his faith & will
To love his life &, worse, he fears
It wouldn't: if he survived that death
He'd somehow never trust a simple life
Or stupid faith in dark again,
All suspect, all fugitive, survivors
On offal. But still he knows he errs
In this—scared & furious at the chance,
Just as, at last, he knows the dark, how it's
Beyond his power or wish to argue—& submits.

When Her Digital Clock

Says 5:55 pigeon knows it's time &
So on Thanksgiving morning he is up,
Appropriately thankful to be
Scratching in his pigeon book on this one,
Old ones, older & older ones:
Something in them still calls him
Out of the bed & brings him along.
One thing not to give thanks for is,
Sixteen years ago today, the young
President's death in Dallas &
All the train of griefs it pulled,
Martin, Bobby, Malcolm & Medger,
Viet Nam & LBJ (who actually said,
Of the war-protesters, "Forgive them, Lord,
For they know not what they do") & also
Watergate & that other one
P won't let into his song at all,
Except (for rhyme) right here—milhous,
The charmless, witless, sexless louse.
Well—despite carps backward & abysms—
Pigeon is giving thanks today: for
The living children, surviving love,
For pages up there on which to write,
For the fat bird in the oven,
For the slender one in his bed,

For all his days & nights with her ahead,
For whatever else it is at 5:55
That gets him up to scratch
The thanking day alive.

This book has been set in Eric Gill's
Joanna & Perpetua types by Graphic Composition, Inc.
and printed by Thomson-Shore, Inc. in an edition
of 1,000 copies, 50 of which have been
numbered & signed by the author.

Design by Jonathan Greene.

Photograph by Harry Connolly.

Roland Flint is the author of six poetry collections: *And Morning, Say It, The Honey and Other Poems for Rosalind, Resuming Green: Selected Poems, Sicily,* and *Stubborn.* He teaches at Georgetown University.